PRESENTED TO:

_____

FROM:

_____

DATE:

_____

On This
CHRISTMAS

A FIVE-YEAR JOURNAL
OF YOUR FAVORITE TRADITIONS,
MEMORIES & GIFTS

ZONDERVAN®

On This Christmas

Copyright © 2018 by Zondervan

Requests for information should be addressed to:
Zondervan, 3900 Sparks Dr., SE, Grand Rapids, MI 49546

ISBN 978-0-3104-5200-3

Cover design: Milkglass Creative
Interior design: Mallory Collins

Printed in China

18 19 20 21 22 23 24 /DSC/ 22 21 20 19 18 17 16 15 14 13 12 11 10 9 8 7 6 5 4 3 2 1

INTRODUCTION

I'll never forget this Christmas!

Even with the best intentions, memories fade, and you lose some of those precious moments in time.

What if you could capture years of those sweet holiday celebrations with family members, the warmth of sharing traditions with the people you love, and the unexpected, thoughtful gifts that delight you? In your hands you hold the answer. A means to keep those memories safely tucked away in the state they were always meant to be—unforgotten.

Curl up on cold December evenings and preserve in writing the things that make this season special to you, whether it's serving others, baking up your family's favorite Christmas cookies, or reaching out to old friends. In the years to come, you'll treasure the words you wrote and be glad you created a cherished book of memories of this most special holiday.

THE BIRTH OF
OUR SAVIOR

This is how the birth of Jesus the Messiah came about: His mother Mary was pledged to be married to Joseph, but before they came together, she was found to be pregnant through the Holy Spirit. Because Joseph her husband was faithful to the law, and yet did not want to expose her to public disgrace, he had in mind to divorce her quietly.

But after he had considered this, an angel of the Lord appeared to him in a dream and said, "Joseph son of David, do not be afraid to take Mary home as your wife, because what is conceived in her is from the Holy Spirit. She will give birth to a son, and you are to give him the name Jesus, because he will save his people from their sins."

All this took place to fulfill what the Lord had said through the prophet: "The virgin will conceive and give birth to a son, and they will call him Immanuel" (which means "God with us").

When Joseph woke up, he did what the angel of the Lord had commanded him and took Mary home as his wife. But he did not consummate their marriage until she gave birth to a son. And he gave him the name Jesus.

Matthew 1:18–25

_____

Year

DECEMBER 1

Describe one of your favorite Christmas traditions, or a new one you'd like to start.

DECEMBER 2

*Which gift are you most
excited to share? Why?*

_____

_____

_____

_____

_____

_____

_____

_____

_____

_____

_____

_____

_____

_____

_____

DECEMBER 3

In what ways are you choosing to slow down the holiday this year?

_____

_____

_____

_____

_____

_____

_____

_____

_____

_____

_____

_____

_____

_____

_____

Our hearts grow tender with childhood memories and love of kindred, and we are better throughout the year for having, in spirit, become a child again at Christmastime.

Laura Ingalls Wilder

DECEMBER 4

What is something you'd like to try this year to keep the focus of Christmas on its true meaning?

_____

_____

_____

_____

_____

_____

_____

_____

_____

_____

_____

_____

_____

_____

_____

_____

DECEMBER 5

If you could invite anyone to spend Christmas with you this year, who would it be? Why?

_____

_____

_____

_____

_____

_____

_____

_____

_____

_____

_____

_____

_____

_____

_____

_____

_____

DECEMBER 6

*Name some ways you can enjoy
Christmas this year the way a child does.*

_____

_____

_____

_____

_____

_____

_____

_____

_____

_____

_____

_____

_____

_____

_____

_____

_____

DECEMBER 7

Who is someone you could connect with this year whom you haven't spoken to in a while?

DECEMBER 8

*What is one thing you
really want for Christmas?*

_____

_____

_____

_____

_____

_____

_____

_____

_____

_____

_____

_____

_____

_____

_____

_____

DECEMBER 9

*What would it just not
be Christmas without?*

_____

_____

_____

_____

_____

_____

_____

_____

_____

_____

_____

_____

_____

_____

_____

_____

_____

DECEMBER 10

*Where and with whom will
you be spending Christmas?*

_____

_____

_____

_____

_____

_____

_____

_____

_____

_____

_____

_____

_____

_____

_____

_____

_____

The Word was God. . . .
The Word became flesh
and made his dwelling
among us.

John 1:1, 14

DECEMBER 11

*What are you doing for
the first time this season?*

_____

_____

_____

_____

_____

_____

_____

_____

_____

_____

_____

_____

_____

_____

_____

DECEMBER 12

*What will your Christmas
dinner menu include this year?*

DECEMBER 13

Describe one of your favorite Christmas tree ornaments. Why is it special to you?

DECEMBER 14

*If you could go anywhere for
Christmas this year, where would you go?*

_____

_____

_____

_____

_____

_____

_____

_____

_____

_____

_____

_____

_____

_____

_____

_____

DECEMBER 15

*What Christmas treats did
you make or enjoy this year?
Share the recipe if you have it.*

_____

_____

_____

_____

_____

_____

_____

_____

_____

_____

_____

_____

_____

_____

DECEMBER 16

What can you do this Christmas season to show gratitude for all that Jesus has done for you?

DECEMBER 17

*How have you seen God's
love at work this month?*

Yet as I read the birth stories about Jesus I cannot help but conclude that though the world may be tilted toward the rich and powerful, God is tilted toward the underdog.

Philip Yancey,
The Jesus I Never Knew

DECEMBER 18

What is the most challenging aspect of the season for you?

_____

_____

_____

_____

_____

_____

_____

_____

_____

_____

_____

_____

_____

_____

_____

_____

_____

_____

_____

DECEMBER 19

What's your favorite way to relax and recharge during this holiday season?

DECEMBER 20

*Whom are you praying
for this Christmas? Why?*

_____

_____

_____

_____

_____

_____

_____

_____

_____

_____

_____

_____

_____

_____

_____

DECEMBER 21

*What is one of the most fun things
to do at Christmas in your town?*

Christmas is a reminder from God Himself that we are not alone. Jesus Christ is here. He is here to give us hope, to forgive our sins, to give us a new song, to impart faith, and to heal our spiritual wounds if only we will let Him.

Billy Graham

DECEMBER 22

Who has inspired you this season?

_____

_____

_____

_____

_____

_____

_____

_____

_____

_____

_____

_____

_____

_____

_____

_____

_____

_____

_____

DECEMBER 23

*Which Christmas movies or shows
did you watch this month, and
which one was your favorite?*

_____

_____

_____

_____

_____

_____

_____

_____

_____

_____

_____

_____

_____

_____

_____

_____

DECEMBER 24

What have you loved most about these days leading up to Christmas?

_____

_____

_____

_____

_____

_____

_____

_____

_____

_____

_____

_____

_____

_____

_____

_____

_____

DECEMBER 25

*Share a favorite Christmas
memory from this year.*

_____

Year

DECEMBER 1

Describe one of your favorite Christmas traditions, or a new one you'd like to start.

_____

_____

_____

_____

_____

_____

_____

_____

_____

_____

_____

_____

_____

_____

_____

_____

_____

DECEMBER 2

*Which gift are you most
excited to share? Why?*

_____

_____

_____

_____

_____

_____

_____

_____

_____

_____

_____

_____

_____

_____

_____

_____

_____

_____

_____

DECEMBER 3

In what ways are you choosing to
slow down the holiday this year?

_____

_____

_____

_____

_____

_____

_____

_____

_____

_____

_____

_____

_____

_____

_____

_____

_____

_____

DECEMBER 4

What is something you'd like to try this year to keep the focus of Christmas on its true meaning?

_____

_____

_____

_____

_____

_____

_____

_____

_____

_____

_____

_____

_____

_____

_____

_____

Christmas is built upon a beautiful and intentional paradox; that the birth of the homeless should be celebrated in every home.

G. K. Chesterton,
Brave New Family

DECEMBER 5

*If you could invite anyone to
spend Christmas with you this
year, who would it be? Why?*

_____

_____

_____

_____

_____

_____

_____

_____

_____

_____

_____

_____

_____

_____

_____

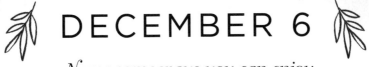

DECEMBER 6

Name some ways you can enjoy
Christmas this year the way a child does.

_____

_____

_____

_____

_____

_____

_____

_____

_____

_____

_____

_____

_____

_____

_____

_____

_____

In those days Caesar Augustus issued a decree that a census should be taken of the entire Roman world. (This was the first census that took place while Quirinius was governor of Syria.) And everyone went to their own town to register.

So Joseph also went up from the town of Nazareth in Galilee to Judea, to Bethlehem the town of David, because he belonged to the house and line of David. He went there to register with Mary, who was pledged to be married to him and was expecting a child. While they were there, the time came for the baby to be born, and she gave birth to her firstborn, a son. She wrapped him in cloths and placed him in a manger, because there was no guest room available for them.

Luke 2:1–7

DECEMBER 7

*Who is someone you could
connect with this year whom
you haven't spoken to in a while?*

_____

_____

_____

_____

_____

_____

_____

_____

_____

_____

_____

_____

_____

_____

_____

DECEMBER 8

*What is one thing you
really want for Christmas?*

DECEMBER 9

What would it just not
be Christmas without?

DECEMBER 10

Where and with whom will you be spending Christmas?

_____

_____

_____

_____

_____

_____

_____

_____

_____

_____

_____

_____

_____

_____

_____

_____

For God so loved the world that he gave his one and only Son, that whoever believes in him shall not perish but have eternal life. For God did not send his Son into the world to condemn the world, but to save the world through him.

John 3:16–17

DECEMBER 11

*What are you doing for
the first time this season?*

_____
_____
_____
_____
_____
_____
_____
_____
_____
_____
_____
_____
_____
_____
_____
_____
_____

DECEMBER 12

*What will your Christmas
dinner menu include this year?*

_____

_____

_____

_____

_____

_____

_____

_____

_____

_____

_____

_____

_____

_____

_____

_____

_____

_____

_____

DECEMBER 13

Describe one of your favorite Christmas tree ornaments. Why is it special to you?

DECEMBER 14

If you could go anywhere for
Christmas this year, where would you go?

_____

_____

_____

_____

_____

_____

_____

_____

_____

_____

_____

_____

_____

_____

_____

_____

_____

_____

DECEMBER 15

*What Christmas treats did
you make or enjoy this year?
Share the recipe if you have it.*

DECEMBER 16

*What can you do this Christmas
season to show gratitude for all
that Jesus has done for you?*

Christmas,

my child,

is love

in action.

Dale Evans Rogers,
A Happy Trails Christmas

DECEMBER 17

How have you seen God's love at work this month?

DECEMBER 18

What is the most challenging aspect of the season for you?

DECEMBER 19

What's your favorite way to relax and recharge during this holiday season?

_____

_____

_____

_____

_____

_____

_____

_____

_____

_____

_____

_____

_____

_____

_____

_____

DECEMBER 20

*Whom are you praying for
this Christmas? Why?*

_____

_____

_____

_____

_____

_____

_____

_____

_____

_____

_____

_____

_____

_____

_____

_____

_____

_____

Christmas is a time of expressing love—God's love—to the people around you, and there is no better way to do so than to tell them about all Jesus did for them. So, to honor the Lord this Christmas and to live out your "thank You" to Him, proclaim the good news of salvation to the people you know.

Charles F. Stanley
Christmas: A Gift for Every Heart

DECEMBER 21

What is one of the most fun things to do at Christmas in your town?

_____

_____

_____

_____

_____

_____

_____

_____

_____

_____

_____

_____

_____

_____

_____

_____

_____

DECEMBER 22

Who has inspired you this season?

DECEMBER 23

*Which Christmas movies or shows
did you watch this month, and
which one was your favorite?*

_____

_____

_____

_____

_____

_____

_____

_____

_____

_____

_____

_____

_____

_____

_____

_____

DECEMBER 24

What have you loved most about
these days leading up to Christmas?

_____

_____

_____

_____

_____

_____

_____

_____

_____

_____

_____

_____

_____

_____

_____

_____

And there were shepherds living out in the fields nearby, keeping watch over their flocks at night. An angel of the Lord appeared to them, and the glory of the Lord shone around them, and they were terrified. But the angel said to them, "Do not be afraid. I bring you good news that will cause great joy for all the people. Today in the town of David a Savior has been born to you; he is the Messiah, the Lord. This will be a sign to you: You will find a baby wrapped in cloths and lying in a manger."

Suddenly a great company of the heavenly host appeared with the angel, praising God and saying, "Glory to God in the highest heaven, and on earth peace to those on whom his favor rests."

Luke 2:8–14

DECEMBER 25

*Share a favorite Christmas
memory from this year.*

_____

Year

DECEMBER 1

Describe one of your favorite Christmas traditions, or a new one you'd like to start.

DECEMBER 2

*Which gift are you most
excited to share? Why?*

_____

_____

_____

_____

_____

_____

_____

_____

_____

_____

_____

_____

_____

_____

_____

_____

_____

DECEMBER 3

*In what ways are you choosing to
slow down the holiday this year?*

_____

_____

_____

_____

_____

_____

_____

_____

_____

_____

_____

_____

_____

_____

_____

DECEMBER 4

What is something you'd like to try this year to keep the focus of Christmas on its true meaning?

DECEMBER 5

If you could invite anyone to spend Christmas with you this year, who would it be? Why?

_____

_____

_____

_____

_____

_____

_____

_____

_____

_____

_____

_____

_____

_____

The rooms were very still while the pages were softly turned and the winter sunshine crept in to touch the bright heads and serious faces with a Christmas greeting.

Louisa May Alcott,
Little Women

DECEMBER 6

Name some ways you can enjoy
Christmas this year the way a child does.

_____

_____

_____

_____

_____

_____

_____

_____

_____

_____

_____

_____

_____

_____

_____

_____

_____

DECEMBER 7

*Who is someone you could
connect with this year whom
you haven't spoken to in a while?*

_____

_____

_____

_____

_____

_____

_____

_____

_____

_____

_____

_____

_____

_____

_____

_____

DECEMBER 8

*What is one thing you
really want for Christmas?*

_____

_____

_____

_____

_____

_____

_____

_____

_____

_____

_____

_____

_____

_____

_____

_____

DECEMBER 9

*What would it just not
be Christmas without?*

DECEMBER 10

Where and with whom will
you be spending Christmas?

_____

_____

_____

_____

_____

_____

_____

_____

_____

_____

_____

_____

_____

_____

_____

_____

Thanks be to
God for his
indescribable gift!

2 Corinthians 9:15

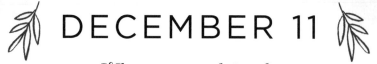

DECEMBER 11

*What are you doing for
the first time this season?*

_____

_____

_____

_____

_____

_____

_____

_____

_____

_____

_____

_____

_____

_____

_____

_____

_____

_____

DECEMBER 12

*What will your Christmas
dinner menu include this year?*

DECEMBER 13

Describe one of your favorite Christmas tree ornaments. Why is it special to you?

_____

_____

_____

_____

_____

_____

_____

_____

_____

_____

_____

_____

_____

_____

_____

_____

DECEMBER 14

*If you could go anywhere for
Christmas this year, where would you go?*

_____

_____

_____

_____

_____

_____

_____

_____

_____

_____

_____

_____

_____

_____

_____

_____

DECEMBER 15

What Christmas treats did you make or enjoy this year? Share the recipe if you have it.

DECEMBER 16

*What can you do this Christmas
season to show gratitude for all
that Jesus has done for you?*

_____

_____

_____

_____

_____

_____

_____

_____

_____

_____

_____

_____

_____

_____

_____

_____

DECEMBER 17

How have you seen God's love at work this month?

DECEMBER 18

*What is the most challenging
aspect of the season for you?*

_____

_____

_____

_____

_____

_____

_____

_____

_____

_____

_____

_____

_____

_____

_____

_____

DECEMBER 19

What's your favorite way to relax and recharge during this holiday season?

_____

_____

_____

_____

_____

_____

_____

_____

_____

_____

_____

_____

_____

_____

_____

_____

_____

For outlandish creatures like us, on our way to a heart, a brain, and courage, Bethlehem is not the end of our journey but only the beginning—not home but the place through which we must pass if ever we are to reach home at last.

Frederick Buechner,
The Magnificent Defeat

DECEMBER 20

Whom are you praying for
this Christmas? Why?

_____

_____

_____

_____

_____

_____

_____

_____

_____

_____

_____

_____

_____

_____

_____

_____

_____

_____

_____

DECEMBER 21

*What is one of the most fun things
to do at Christmas in your town?*

DECEMBER 22

Who has inspired you this season?

_____

_____

_____

_____

_____

_____

_____

_____

_____

_____

_____

_____

_____

_____

_____

_____

_____

_____

_____

_____

When the angels had left them and gone into heaven, the shepherds said to one another, "Let's go to Bethlehem and see this thing that has happened, which the Lord has told us about."

So they hurried off and found Mary and Joseph, and the baby, who was lying in the manger. When they had seen him, they spread the word concerning what had been told them about this child, and all who heard it were amazed at what the shepherds said to them. But Mary treasured up all these things and pondered them in her heart. The shepherds returned, glorifying and praising God for all the things they had heard and seen, which were just as they had been told.

Luke 2:15–20

DECEMBER 23

Which Christmas movies or shows
did you watch this month, and
which one was your favorite?

DECEMBER 24

What have you loved most about
these days leading up to Christmas?

_____

_____

_____

_____

_____

_____

_____

_____

_____

_____

_____

_____

_____

_____

_____

_____

_____

_____

_____

DECEMBER 25

*Share a favorite Christmas
memory from this year.*

Year

DECEMBER 1

Describe one of your favorite Christmas traditions, or a new one you'd like to start.

_____

_____

_____

_____

_____

_____

_____

_____

_____

_____

_____

_____

_____

_____

DECEMBER 2

*Which gift are you most
excited to share? Why?*

_____
_____
_____
_____
_____
_____
_____
_____
_____
_____
_____
_____
_____
_____
_____
_____
_____
_____
_____

DECEMBER 3

In what ways are you choosing to slow down the holiday this year?

_____

_____

_____

_____

_____

_____

_____

_____

_____

_____

_____

_____

_____

_____

_____

_____

DECEMBER 4

What is something you'd like to try this year to keep the focus of Christmas on its true meaning?

_____

_____

_____

_____

_____

_____

_____

_____

_____

_____

_____

_____

_____

_____

_____

_____

Christmas is the season for
kindling the fire of hospitality
in the hall, the genial flame
of charity in the heart.

Washington Irving,
Old Christmas

DECEMBER 5

If you could invite anyone to spend Christmas with you this year, who would it be? Why?

_____

_____

_____

_____

_____

_____

_____

_____

_____

_____

_____

_____

_____

_____

_____

_____

_____

DECEMBER 6

*Name some ways you can enjoy
Christmas this year the way a child does.*

_____

_____

_____

_____

_____

_____

_____

_____

_____

_____

_____

_____

_____

_____

_____

_____

_____

DECEMBER 7

Who is someone you could
connect with this year whom
you haven't spoken to in a while?

_____

_____

_____

_____

_____

_____

_____

_____

_____

_____

_____

_____

_____

_____

DECEMBER 8

*What is one thing you
really want for Christmas?*

_____

_____

_____

_____

_____

_____

_____

_____

_____

_____

_____

_____

_____

_____

_____

_____

_____

DECEMBER 9

*What would it just not
be Christmas without?*

_____

_____

_____

_____

_____

_____

_____

_____

_____

_____

_____

_____

_____

_____

_____

_____

DECEMBER 10

Where and with whom will
you be spending Christmas?

_____

_____

_____

_____

_____

_____

_____

_____

_____

_____

_____

_____

_____

_____

_____

_____

This is how God showed his love among us: He sent his one and only Son into the world that we might live through him.

1 John 4:9

DECEMBER 11

*What are you doing for
the first time this season?*

_____

_____

_____

_____

_____

_____

_____

_____

_____

_____

_____

_____

_____

_____

_____

DECEMBER 12

*What will your Christmas
dinner menu include this year?*

_____

_____

_____

_____

_____

_____

_____

_____

_____

_____

_____

_____

_____

_____

_____

_____

_____

_____

DECEMBER 13

Describe one of your favorite Christmas tree ornaments. Why is it special to you?

_____

_____

_____

_____

_____

_____

_____

_____

_____

_____

_____

_____

_____

_____

_____

_____

DECEMBER 14

*If you could go anywhere for
Christmas this year, where would you go?*

_____

_____

_____

_____

_____

_____

_____

_____

_____

_____

_____

_____

_____

_____

_____

_____

_____

I heard the bells
on Christmas Day
Their old, familiar
carols play,
And wild and sweet
The words repeat
Of peace on earth,
good-will to men!

Henry Wadsworth Longfellow,
"Christmas Bells"

DECEMBER 15

*What Christmas treats did
you make or enjoy this year?
Share the recipe if you have it.*

_____

_____

_____

_____

_____

_____

_____

_____

_____

_____

_____

_____

_____

_____

_____

_____

_____

_____

_____

DECEMBER 16

What can you do this Christmas season to show gratitude for all that Jesus has done for you?

DECEMBER 17

*How have you seen God's
love at work this month?*

DECEMBER 18

What is the most challenging
aspect of the season for you?

_____

_____

_____

_____

_____

_____

_____

_____

_____

_____

_____

_____

_____

_____

_____

_____

_____

DECEMBER 19

What's your favorite way to relax and recharge during this holiday season?

_____

_____

_____

_____

_____

_____

_____

_____

_____

_____

_____

_____

_____

_____

_____

_____

_____

DECEMBER 20

Whom are you praying for
this Christmas? Why?

DECEMBER 21

*What is one of the most fun things
to do at Christmas in your town?*

_____

_____

_____

_____

_____

_____

_____

_____

_____

_____

_____

_____

_____

_____

_____

_____

DECEMBER 22

Who has inspired you this season?

_____

_____

_____

_____

_____

_____

_____

_____

_____

_____

_____

_____

_____

_____

_____

_____

_____

_____

DECEMBER 23

*Which Christmas movies or shows
did you watch this month, and
which one was your favorite?*

_____

_____

_____

_____

_____

_____

_____

_____

_____

_____

_____

_____

_____

_____

_____

The Lord God will give him the throne of his father David, and . . . his kingdom will never end.

Luke 1:32–33

DECEMBER 24

What have you loved most about these days leading up to Christmas?

_____

_____

_____

_____

_____

_____

_____

_____

_____

_____

_____

_____

_____

_____

_____

_____

DECEMBER 25

Share a favorite Christmas memory from this year.

Year

DECEMBER 1

Describe one of your favorite Christmas traditions, or a new one you'd like to start.

_____

_____

_____

_____

_____

_____

_____

_____

_____

_____

_____

_____

_____

_____

_____

_____

DECEMBER 2

*Which gift are you most
excited to share? Why?*

_____

_____

_____

_____

_____

_____

_____

_____

_____

_____

_____

_____

_____

_____

_____

_____

_____

DECEMBER 3

In what ways are you choosing to slow down the holiday this year?

_____

_____

_____

_____

_____

_____

_____

_____

_____

_____

_____

_____

_____

_____

_____

_____

_____

DECEMBER 4

*What is something you'd like to
try this year to keep the focus of
Christmas on its true meaning?*

_____

_____

_____

_____

_____

_____

_____

_____

_____

_____

_____

_____

_____

_____

_____

_____

Christmas is not a time or
a season but a state of mind.
To cherish peace and good will,
to be plenteous in mercy,
is to have the real spirit of Christmas.

Calvin Coolidge

DECEMBER 5

If you could invite anyone to spend Christmas with you this year, who would it be? Why?

_____

_____

_____

_____

_____

_____

_____

_____

_____

_____

_____

_____

_____

_____

_____

_____

_____

DECEMBER 6

Name some ways you can enjoy
Christmas this year the way a child does.

_____

_____

_____

_____

_____

_____

_____

_____

_____

_____

_____

_____

_____

_____

_____

_____

_____

_____

DECEMBER 7

Who is someone you could connect with this year whom you haven't spoken to in a while?

_____

_____

_____

_____

_____

_____

_____

_____

_____

_____

_____

_____

_____

_____

_____

DECEMBER 8

*What is one thing you
really want for Christmas?*

_____
_____
_____
_____
_____
_____
_____
_____
_____
_____
_____
_____
_____
_____
_____
_____
_____

DECEMBER 9

*What would it just not
be Christmas without?*

_____

_____

_____

_____

_____

_____

_____

_____

_____

_____

_____

_____

_____

_____

_____

_____

DECEMBER 10

*Where and with whom will
you be spending Christmas?*

_____
_____
_____
_____
_____
_____
_____
_____
_____
_____
_____
_____
_____
_____
_____
_____
_____

For to us a child is born,
to us a son is given,
and the government
will be on his shoulders.
And he will be called
Wonderful Counselor, Mighty God,
Everlasting Father, Prince of Peace.

Isaiah 9:6

DECEMBER 11

*What are you doing for
the first time this season?*

_____

_____

_____

_____

_____

_____

_____

_____

_____

_____

_____

_____

_____

_____

_____

_____

_____

DECEMBER 12

*What will your Christmas
dinner menu include this year?*

_____

_____

_____

_____

_____

_____

_____

_____

_____

_____

_____

_____

_____

_____

_____

_____

_____

DECEMBER 13

Describe one of your favorite Christmas tree ornaments. Why is it special to you?

_____

_____

_____

_____

_____

_____

_____

_____

_____

_____

_____

_____

_____

_____

_____

_____

_____

DECEMBER 14

If you could go anywhere for
Christmas this year, where would you go?

_____

_____

_____

_____

_____

_____

_____

_____

_____

_____

_____

_____

_____

_____

_____

_____

_____

DECEMBER 15

*What Christmas treats did
you make or enjoy this year?
Share the recipe if you have it.*

_____

_____

_____

_____

_____

_____

_____

_____

_____

_____

_____

_____

_____

_____

_____

_____

DECEMBER 16

What can you do this Christmas season to show gratitude for all that Jesus has done for you?

DECEMBER 17

*How have you seen God's
love at work this month?*

_____

_____

_____

_____

_____

_____

_____

_____

_____

_____

_____

_____

_____

_____

_____

_____

_____

_____

The only blind
person at Christmas
time is he who
has not Christmas
in his heart.

Helen Keller
"Christmas in the Dark,"
Ladies Home Journal

DECEMBER 18

*What is the most challenging
aspect of the season for you?*

_____

_____

_____

_____

_____

_____

_____

_____

_____

_____

_____

_____

_____

_____

_____

_____

_____

_____

_____

DECEMBER 19

What's your favorite way to relax and recharge during this holiday season?

_____

_____

_____

_____

_____

_____

_____

_____

_____

_____

_____

_____

_____

_____

_____

_____

_____

_____

_____

DECEMBER 20

*Whom are you praying
for this Christmas? Why?*

_____

_____

_____

_____

_____

_____

_____

_____

_____

_____

_____

_____

_____

_____

_____

_____

_____

_____

_____

DECEMBER 21

What is one of the most fun things
to do at Christmas in your town?

_____

_____

_____

_____

_____

_____

_____

_____

_____

_____

_____

_____

_____

_____

_____

_____

DECEMBER 22

Who has inspired you this season?

_____

_____

_____

_____

_____

_____

_____

_____

_____

_____

_____

_____

_____

_____

_____

_____

_____

_____

_____

DECEMBER 23

*Which Christmas movies or shows
did you watch this month, and
which one was your favorite?*

_____

_____

_____

_____

_____

_____

_____

_____

_____

_____

_____

_____

_____

_____

_____

_____

_____

DECEMBER 24

*What have you loved most about
these days leading up to Christmas?*

_____

_____

_____

_____

_____

_____

_____

_____

_____

_____

_____

_____

_____

_____

_____

_____